ZAWA (MURMUR)
ZAWA
ZAWA
KA (CLACK)
KA
KA

ZA (STEP)

3
THE BOY & THE BEAST
original story by
Mamoru Hosoda
art by
Renji Asai
©2015 B.B.F.P

PATH

THE BOY & THE BEAST

original story by
Mamoru Hosoda
art by
Renji Asai

3

CONTENTS

IMPOSSIBLE, I'LL SAY.

HUH?

I HAVE NO IDEA WHAT KIND OF STUDENT YOU ARE ...
...BUT IF YOU'VE BEEN OUT OF SCHOOL ALL THIS TIME, THEN WHY NOT JUST START TAKING CLASSES AT A NIGHTTIME MIDDLE SCHOOL?
UM, BUT...
LIFE JUST ISN'T THAT EASY, YOU KNOW.

EVEN IF YOU DID MANAGE TO PASS THE EXAMS, WHAT WILL YOU DO ABOUT TUITION WITHOUT A GUARDIAN'S SUPPORT?
YOU CAN'T GET MUCH IN THE WAY OF SCHOLARSHIPS THESE DAYS UNLESS YOU'RE AN EXCEPTIONAL STUDENT.

EXCUSE ME!
THIS IS WHERE WE CAN GET INFORMATION, ISN'T IT?

YES, AND THAT'S WHAT I'M GIVING YOU...
GUGUGU (STRAIN)

WE'VE HEARD ENOUGH!
THANK YOU VERY MUCH!!!
GATAN (THUNK)

ZUKKA (STOMP)
ZUKKA

THIS COLLEGE THING JUST ISN'T GOING TO WORK...
WHAT'S HIS PROBLEM!? I'M SO PISSED!!

OH... OKAY.

U-UM...!

ZUI (LEAN)

THANK YOU VERY MUCH!!

GABA (BOW)

THANK YOU... VERY MUCH.

PARA (FLIP)
I HAVE TO STUDY MATH AND SCIENCE TOO... I HAVEN'T TOUCHED THOSE AT ALL.
IT'S OKAY. YOU'LL BE JUST FINE.
NAME
ITEMS
1 REQUIRED
1 ONE OF TWO SUBJECTS REQUIRED.
1 ONE OF FOUR SUBJECTS REQUIRED.
1 OR 2 "MODERN SOCIETY" OR "ETHICS" AND "GOVERNMENT AND ECONOMICS" REQUIRED
REQUIRED
1 EITHER 1 OR 2 BELOW IS REQUIRED

I'M NOT SO SURE.
LEAVE IT TO ME. I'LL MAKE SURE YOU PASS!

POON (BONG)
...IN ORDER TO TAKE THE HIGH SCHOOL EQUIVALENCY EXAM, YOU NEED A CITIZEN IDENTIFICATION CARD.
UNFORTUNATELY, IT SEEMS YOUR PREVIOUS CARD HAS BEEN OFFICIALLY REVOKED.
I FIGURED...
7
HOWEVER, WE STILL HAVE YOU ON RECORD IN THE FAMILY REGISTER, SO IT WOULD BE POSSIBLE TO ISSUE YOU A NEW CARD.

I HAD NO CLUE WHERE HE WAS.

YOU HAVEN'T BEEN...

...LIVING WITH YOUR FATHER, RIGHT...?

I NEVER ...
... THOUGHT I'D FIND HIM THIS EASILY.

ARE YOU GOING TO GO SEE HIM?

IF I JUST SHOW UP...
...IT'LL BE A HASSLE FOR HIM...
REALLY?
HE MIGHT NOT EVEN REMEMBER ME...

BUT...

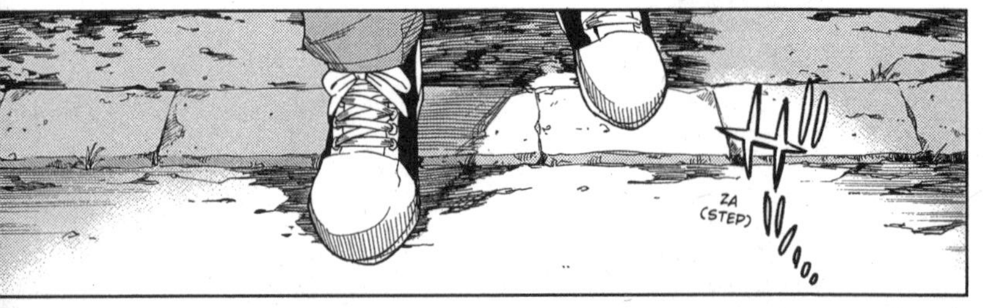
ZA
(STEP)

Paking
24
Paking
24

SU
(REACH)

だらん…
DARAN
(DROP)

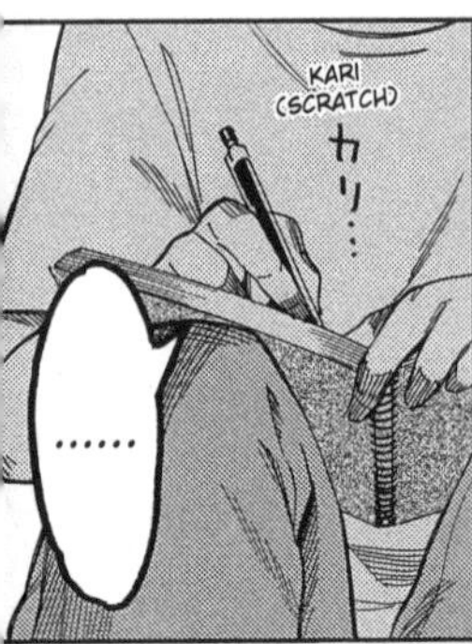

WHAT AM I SUPPOSED TO WRITE ...?

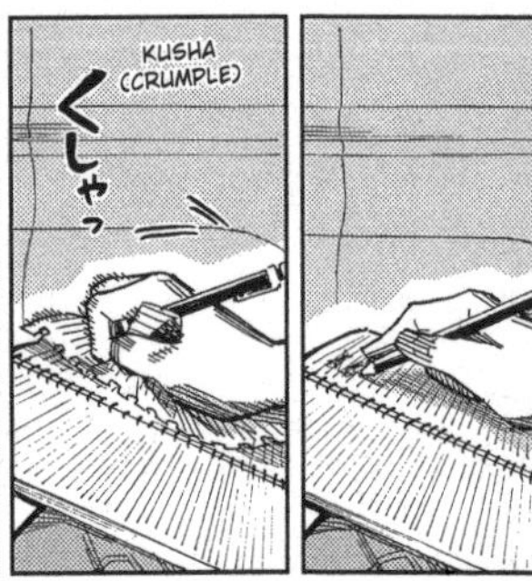

DAD, THROW THE BALL!
TA (STEP)
TA
ZA (STEP)
HA-HA-HA... THERE!
AH HA HA!
CAREFUL.
WATCH WHERE YOU'RE GOING.

GAYA (BUSTLE)
EVE-NING!
WHAT SHOULD WE HAVE FOR DINNER?
GAYA
I'LL THROW THIS IN TOO!
GAYA

THANK YOU.

DAD!

WHAT IS IT, REN?

......!

いせや

SHOES
革化
......
UH...

......
......

...YES?

...UH.
DO...
...YOU... REMEMBER...
...ME...?

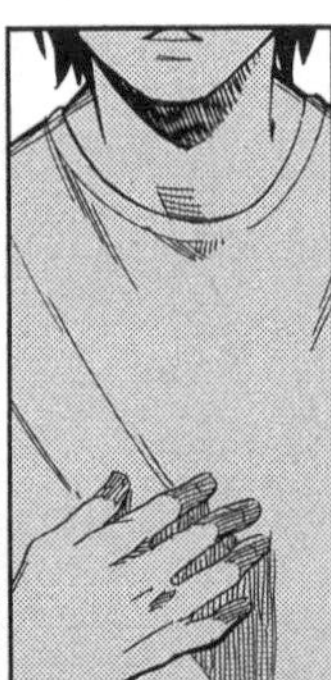

I FIGURED ...

HURRY UP!
BATA (THUD)
BATA
LET'S GO BATTLE OVER THERE!
OKAY!
BATA

BASA
(FLOP)
REN.

ARE YOU REN ...?

!

REN
!!!!

......I'M SO GLAD...

...YOU'RE ALL RIGHT!!!

...REN!!

REN—

...DAD.

DAD...

...SAID THAT HE FOUND OUT ABOUT MOM'S ACCIDENT A LONG TIME AFTER IT HAPPENED.

HE KEPT LOOKING FOR ME AFTER I WENT MISSING.

HE EVEN KEPT LOOKING AROUND AFTER THE POLICE GAVE UP ON ME.

: PATA (DASH) PATA PATA

YEAH.

WHERE WERE YA?

...WE NEED TO TALK. AND I WANT YOU TO ACTUALLY LISTEN TO ME.

WHAT ABOUT YOUR TRAINING?
...JUST LISTEN. THE TRUTH IS—
SO YOU THINK YOU CAN JUST SKIP OUT ON THAT?
HEAR HIM OUT, KUMA-TETSU.
ギロ
GIRO (GLARE)

I WANT TO GO TO A HUMAN SCHOOL.

HUH?
I WANT TO LEARN ABOUT OTHER PLACES.
DON'T YOU HAVE BETTER THINGS TO WORRY ABOUT?
AREN'T YA TRYING TO GET STRONGER?
I HAVE GOTTEN STRONG-ER.
HUH? DON'T MAKE ME LAUGH.

I'VE...
...GOTTEN PLENTY STRONG.

GATAN (CLATTER)
!

WHAT MAKES YOU THINK YOU'RE SO STRONG !?

HUH !?

THIS IS WHAT ALWAYS HAPPENS WHEN I TRY TO TALK TO YOU.

YOU NEVER LISTEN. YOU JUST START YELLING.

OUT WITH IT!! WHEN DID YOU GET SO STRONG !?

......

ZA (GRAB)

ENOUGH.

FINE.

THERE'S ONE MORE THING I HAVE TO TELL YOU.

WHERE'RE YOU GOING!?
WAIT!

I FOUND MY DAD.
I'M GOING TO HIM.

I JUST DECIDED ON THAT.

GATATA (CLATTER)
GII (CREAK)

I WON'T LET YA GO!!!

WAH!
HYU (WHOOSH)

DAAN (SLAM)

DA (DASH)

...!

DON'T GO!!!

CHAPTER 9 END

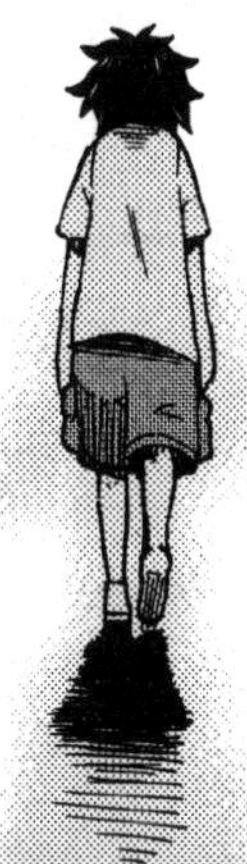

Chapter 10 What's Welling Up Inside of Me

SO, YOU DIDN'T SETTLE WHATEVER WAS BOTHERING YOU.

IT DOESN'T MATTER.
NOT ANYMORE.

I'M OFF TO GO SEE MY DAD.
I'LL SEE HIM, AND THEN I'LL SETTLE THINGS.

DON'T YOU THINK YOU'RE PUSHING YOURSELF?

WHY WOULD I BE?

YOU GET IT, DON'T YOU? YOU WILL IF YOU'RE SMART!

SORRY!!

DON'T JUST APOLOGIZE FOR EVERYTHING!!

SORRY!!!

I KNEW IT.

WITHOUT KYUTA—

GU (GRIP)

SHUT YOUR TRAPS !!!
HYUN (WHOOSH)
WAH!!

ZUKA
ZUKA (STOMP)
WHAT DO YOU THINK YOU'RE DOING !?
THAT'S DANGEROUS!

BA (SHOVE)

...IT'S NOT LIKE I DON'T UNDERSTAND.
?

IN HIS OWN WAY...
...HE WAS TRYING TO BE A PARENT TO KYUTA...
JIWA (CHIRP)
JIWA

...REN!

WE'RE HAVING OMELETS WITH HAM FOR DINNER TONIGHT!
I'LL COOK, SO LET'S EAT TOGETHER!
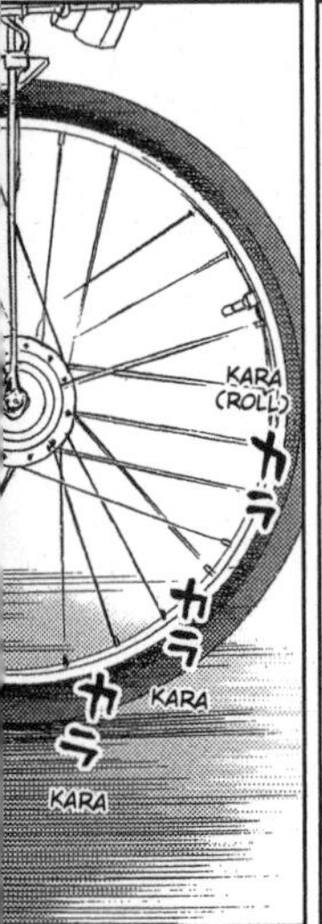
KARA (ROLL)
KARA
KARA

...ONCE I'VE PROPERLY THANKED THEM, YOU SHOULD COME LIVE WITH ME.

...!

...WAIT A MINUTE!

?

WHAT'S WRONG? ...REN?

WELL ...

...SO SUDDENLY ...
WE CAN'T FILL THE GAP IN TIME...
......I SEE.
I GUESS YOU'RE RIGHT. TIME WORKS DIFFERENTLY FOR ADULTS AND KIDS.
THE TIME I SPENT WITH YOU AND YOUR MOM...
...FEELS LIKE ONLY YESTERDAY TO ME...
YES-TERDAY ...
SORRY FOR RUSHING YOU.

LET'S TAKE OUR TIME STARTING OVER.
LET'S TRY TO FORGET ALL THE BAD THINGS OF THE PAST...
...AND WORK TOWARD THE FUTURE...

REN...
YOU DON'T ...
...EVEN KNOW ME...
REN, I...
YOU...
...DON'T KNOW ANYTHING ...
SO DON'T ACT...
...LIKE YOU DO !!!!

GATATA (CLATTER)
......
REN...
HA-HA!

GATATA
WHAT? YOU'VE GOTTA BE KIDDING ME!
GIKO (CLUNK)
GIKO
SERI-OUSLY!
YESTER-DAY AT SCHOOL ...
AH-HA-HA-HA-HA-HA ...

...SORRY.
OF COURSE YOU DON'T KNOW. I HAVEN'T TOLD YOU ANYTHING.

I'LL...
...PASS ON COMING OVER TODAY...
ZA (STEP)

OH ...!
GACHA (CLATTER)

...REN!
TA (STEP)
WH-WHAT ABOUT DINNER ...!?
KARA (ROLL)
KARA
KARA
GATAN (CLUNK)

I'M FINE.
PITA (STOP)
KARARA

YOU CAN DECIDE WHAT IT IS...

...YOU WANT TO DO FROM NOW ON!

I'LL DO EVERYTHING I CAN TO HELP YOU GET THERE!!

WHAT...
WHAT AM I UP TO?
WHY DID I...
...SAY ALL THAT TO DAD?

DON'T GO!!

DAMN IT...!
WHY AM I THINKING ABOUT HIM?

KYUTAAAAAA!!

...DON'T GO!!!

GAYA (BUSTLE)
BUOO (VROOM)
GAYA

HAH.
HAAH ...
HAA.

HAA...
HAH.

!

BUOON
HATE YOU.
BOYA (MUTTER)

I...
... HATE YOU ...

I HATE YOU...
I...
...HATE YOU.

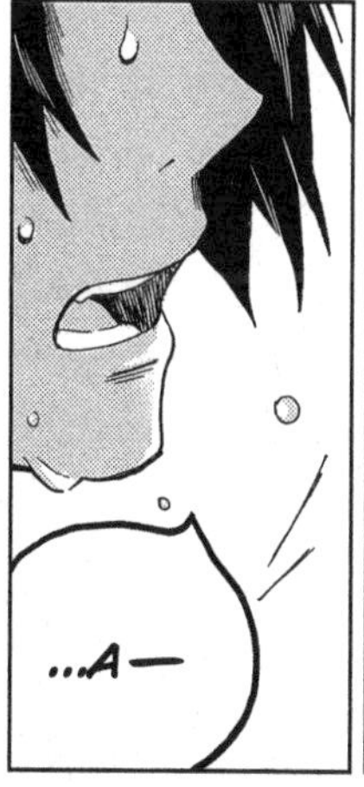

A HOLE ...?

FURA (STUMBLE)

3F
2F

AAAH
—
AHH
...!?
AHH...
......

BA
(GRAB)

......
OO
(RUMBLE)
...IS
THIS
!?
WHAT...
—
AAAHHH
...!!
AAA—
......!!
FURA
(STUMBLE)

SIGN: SHIBUYA PUBLIC LIBRARY

GASHA
GASHA
GASHA
REN-KUN...?

YOU LOOK REALLY SCARY...

...ALMOST LIKE YOU'RE NOT YOU...

...HUMAN?
...OR...
...AM I A
BEAST...?
A BEAST?
WHAT ARE
YOU TALKING
ABOUT...?

TELL ME...
... PLEASE?
REN-KUN.
YOU'RE NOT ACTING LIKE YOURSELF ...!
GASHAN (CLATTER)
!

GASHAN

!!

WHAT ...

...AM I...!?
......
GU (GRIP)
...!
PASHI! (SMACK)
FURA (STUMBLE)

SOMETIMES
...

KASHAN
(CLATTER)

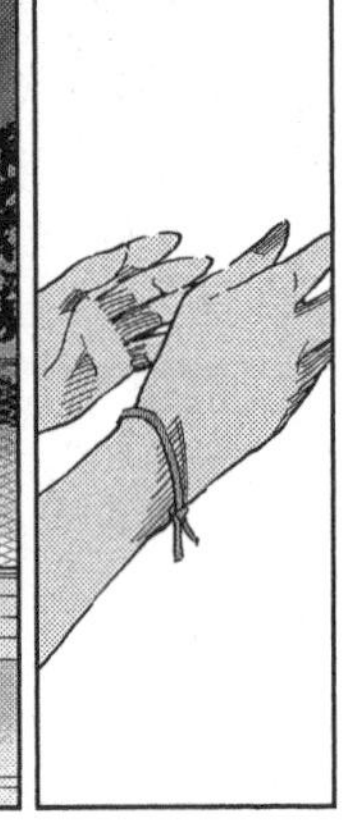

...I
FEEL THIS
INCREDIBLE
AMOUNT OF
PAIN TOO.
LIKE
I JUST
WANT THE
WORLD TO
END.
LIKE
SOMETHING
IS ABOUT TO
COME GUSHING
OUT FROM
INSIDE OF ME...

BUT
I'M
SURE
...
...IT'S NOT
JUST YOU
AND ME WHO
FEEL THAT.
EVERYONE
DOES...

SO IT'S ALL RIGHT.

IT'S OKAY...

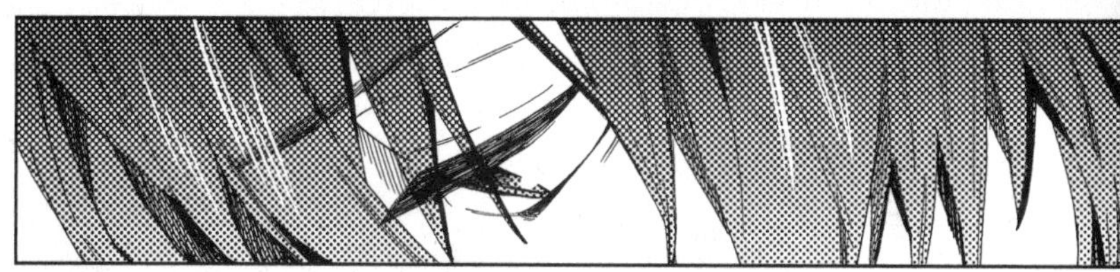

YOU'RE BACK TO THE USUAL YOU.

CHAPTER 10 END

……
ぐっ…
GU (GRIP)
…!

THE BOY & THE BEAST

Chapter II THE DECIDING DAY

BUOOO
(VROOM)
ZAWA
(MURMUR)
ZAWA

ZAWA
ZAWA

THIS...
...WAS MY FAVORITE BOOKMARK WHEN I WAS LITTLE.
SHURU
(BITE)
IT'S REALLY HELPED ME OUT A LOT.
SURU
(SLIP)

KYU (TUG)
IF YOU EVER THINK YOU'RE IN TROUBLE...
...OR START FEELING LIKE YOU DID JUST NOW...
...JUST REMEMBER THIS...IT'LL PROTECT YOU.

GU (GRIP)

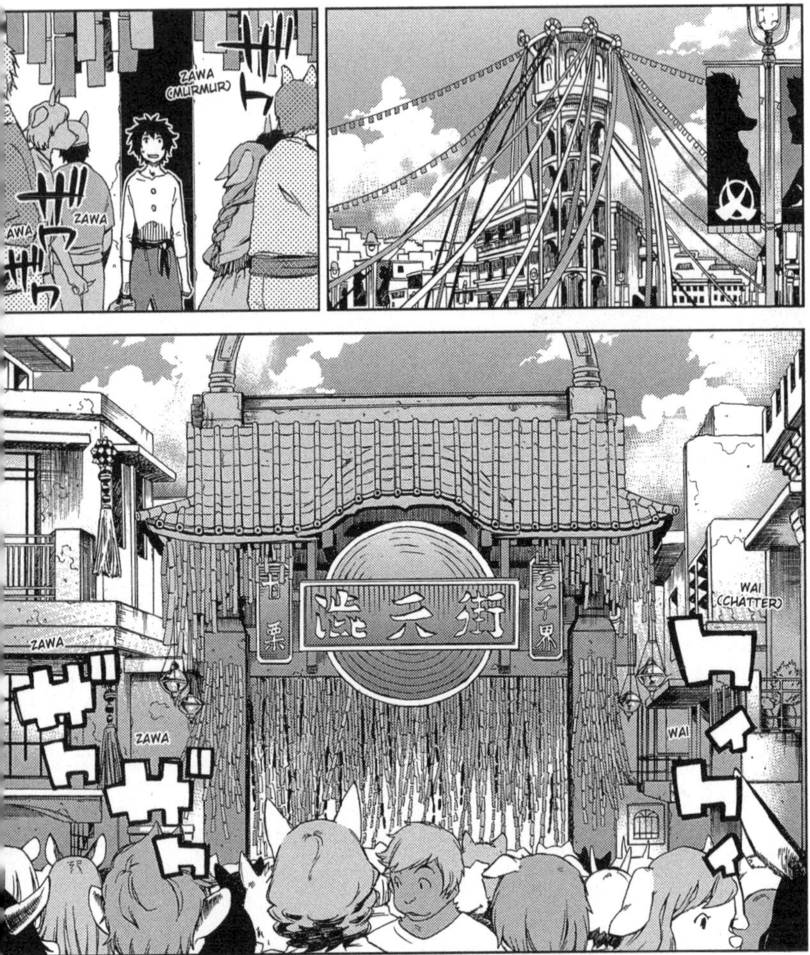

WAI (CHATTER)

WAI

ZAWA

ZAWA

SIGNS (RIGHT TO LEFT): PARADISE, JUTENGAI, SWEET CHESTNUTS

COME ON OVER TO MY PLACE!

THE GRANDMASTER SUDDENLY DECIDED ON THE DAY...
... SO THE ENTIRE TOWN'S TALKING ABOUT IT.
THE DAY?
KATA (CLINK)

TAKE YOUR TIME.
PEKO (BOW)
THANKS, MOM.

...TOMORROW'S THE BIG DAY FOR MY DAD AND YOUR MASTER.
THE MATCH TO SEE WHO'LL BE THE NEW LEADER.
DON'T TELL ME YOU DIDN'T KNOW?

Y'KNOW I...

...HAVEN'T SEEN DAD FOR A BIT NOW EITHER.

HE'S BEEN BUSY TRAINING.

IT'S LONELY, BUT IT CAN'T BE HELPED.

'COS I WANT HIM TO WIN.

KYUTA.

YOU...
...DON'T WANT YOUR MASTER TO LOSE EITHER, DO YOU?

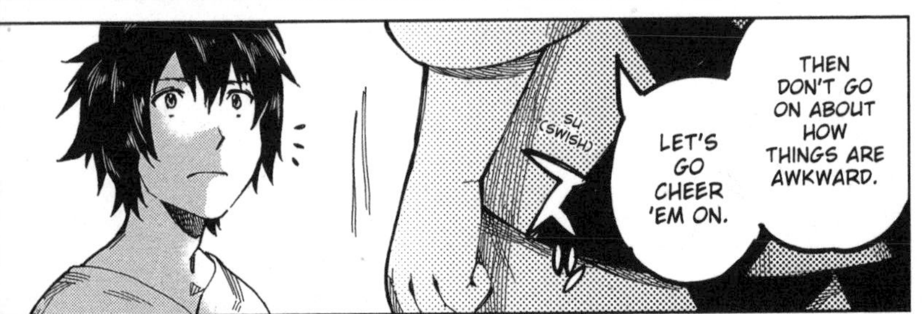
THEN DON'T GO ON ABOUT HOW THINGS ARE AWKWARD.
LET'S GO CHEER 'EM ON.
SU (SWISH)

WHATEVER HAPPENS, WE'RE STILL FRIENDS.
SU (REACH)
OF COURSE.
YEAH.

I HOPE IT'S A GOOD MATCH.
YEAH.

HEH HEH HEH ...

OH.

JIRO-MARU...

BIG BRO!
DON'T DRAG THINGS OUT...
...AND CAUSE TROUBLE FOR KYUTA, OKAY?

KYUTA.

THERE, SEE? THE CICADAS ARE STARTING TO BUZZ.
KANA (BZZ)
KANA
KANA
KA

I'LL SEE YOU OUT.
KANA
KANA
KANA

KANA
KANA
KANA
THEN...
THANKS.

ふわっ
FUWA (FLOAT)

HYU (WHOOSH)

!!

HYU

SLICE

HYUN

ZA (RUSH)

ICHIROHIKO...!

OO (FWOO)

DOSU
(WHAM)
UGH
...
SHU
(SWISH)

DOSU
(WHAM)

GAKUN
(SLUMP)

DO
(THUD)

UGH
...

GEH.

UGH.

......

WHAT'S ALL...
...THIS "GOOD MATCH" STUFF?
GA (THUD)
THE WINNER HAS BEEN DECIDED FROM THE BEGINNING!
GASU (WHAM)
GASU
HUMANS LIKE YOU...
...AND HALF-WITS LIKE KUMA-TETSU...
GASU

GASU
...SHOULD ACT LIKE PROPER HALF-WITS...
...AND KNOW YOUR PLACE!!!
GASU
GASU

GA
GA
ICHIROHIKO
...
I—
GA
HAH,
HAH,
GA

UGH
...
......
パラッ
PARA
(CLATTER

HAA
...
HAA
...

......
HMPH!

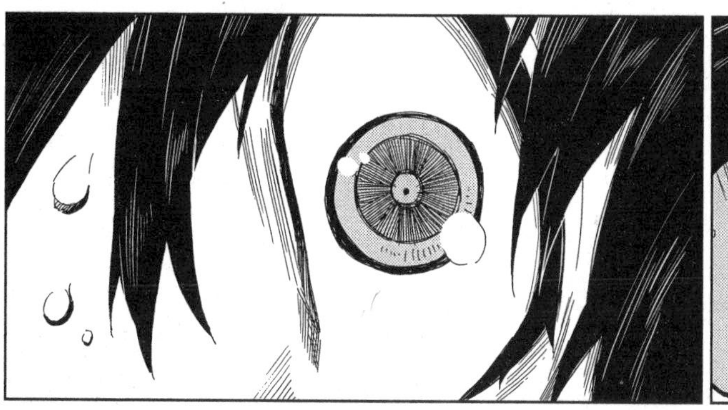

OOOOOO
(RUMBLE)

...A HOLE ...

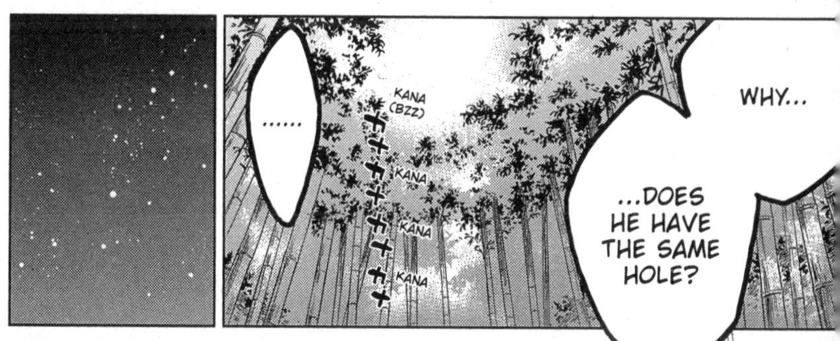

HATA (RATTLE)
ハタハタ...
HATA
OOO (RUMBLE)
WAAAHHH...
OOOO

WAA
WHO ARE YOU ROOTING FOR?
I'M GOING FOR IOZEN.
I'M FOR KUMA-TETSU.
KUMA-TETSU'S GONNA WIN!
NO WAY. IT'S GONNA BE IOZEN!
ZAWA (MURMUR)
ZAWA
I'M IN FOR IOZEN.
I'M GOING FOR KUMA-TETSU.

I'M...
......!
I'M...

...AHH! I JUST DON'T KNOW!
It took me a while!
!
For the past nine years, I've given it endless thought!

But, I've finally made my decision.

SO, WHAT SORT OF GOD ARE YOU GOING TO BE?

None other...

SFX: GOKURI (GULP)

The rites of reincarnation will take place after the match, so look forward to that.
WAAAH...
WAAAH
PYOKO (PEEK)
KYU!

But first...

ZA (STEP)
OOOOOOO (RUMBLE)

OOO
OOO
OOO
ZA (STEP)
OOOO

HEY.
DON'T LOOK SO DOWN IN THE DUMPS. YOU'RE ABOUT TO FIGHT, YOU KNOW.

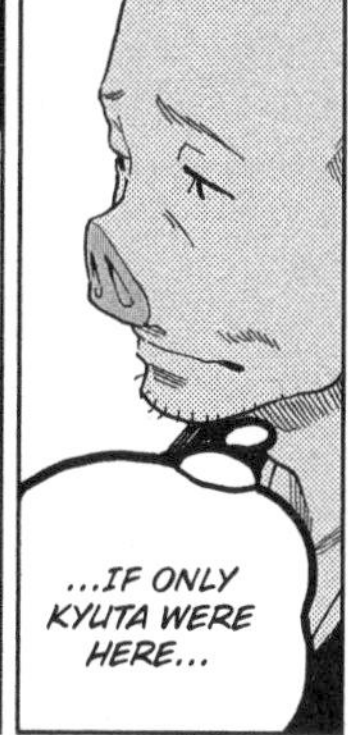
...IF ONLY KYUTA WERE HERE...

ZA

AAAAAARRRGH!

WAH! TOO LOUD!

ARRRRRRRRGH!

ぐっ…
GU
(GRIP)

SU
(LEAN)
Ready yourselves ...!!!

DON (CRUSH)
Begin !!!!
CHAPTER 11 END

THE BOY & THE BEAST

He who falls unconscious for the count of ten, loses.
As always, be sure to act within the rules of etiquette!
Ready yourselves ...
Begin !!!
DON (RUSH)
!?
HEY, NOW ...
!
DA (THUD)
DA
DA
DA

BUKU
(BRISTLE)

BAGAN (RIP)
ISN'T IT TOO SOON FOR THAT !?
CHAPTER 12 FIGHTING ALONE

GRAAAAA!!!
BUOOOO (WHOOSH)
GA (WHAM)
HYUN (WHOOSH)
!
DOSHI (WHUMP)
ZA (SKID)

BUO (WHOOSH)

ZUN (WHUMP)

OOOOO (RUMBLE)

HE DOESN'T KNOW HOW TO PACE HIMSELF...

KUMA-TETSU IS PRESSING IN?

......

THAT IDIOT.

DOSHIII (WHUMP)

ZA (SKID)

ZA

ZA

ZA

ZA

DON (THUD)

DAD!

SHUT UP. JUST BE QUIET AND WATCH!!

もう

MOU (HAZY)

もう

MOU

SU (SWISH)
CHA (CLACK)
DO (THUD)
DO
DO
DO
DO
DO
DO
HYUN (WHOOSH)
BACHI (SMACK)

ザッ
ザッ
ZA (SKID)
ZA
ドッ
ドッ
ドッ
ドッ
DO
DO (THUD)
DO
DO
トッ
TON (TMP)
ドッ
BA (WHOOSH)
オォォォ
WHOOOA!
THERE, SEE!?
オォォォ
WHOOA!

ZA
ザザ
ZA
もぅ
MOU
もぅ
MOU
(HAZY)
バッ
BA
......!

ダッ
DA
(DASH)

AAAAAAHHH!!!

DO (THUD)
GORO (ROLL)
GORO

AHH...!!
OOOOO (RUMBLE)

MOU (HAZY)
MOU
DAMN IT!

DO
DO
DO
GASP!
DO
DO

DO
DO
DO
DO
(THUD)
GABA
(JUMP)

SUKA
(WHOOSH)

HUH
!?
MOTATA
(FLAIL)
DO
!?

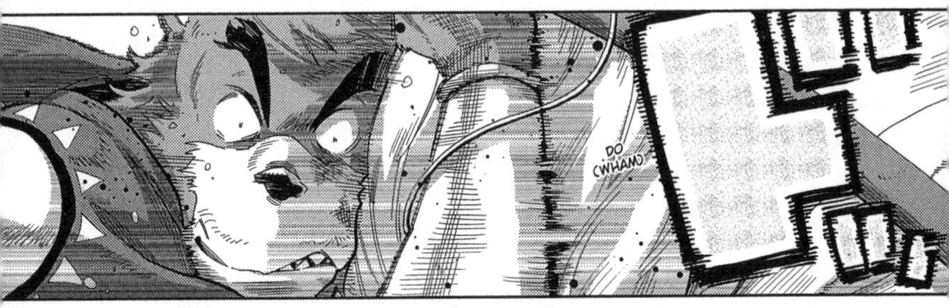
DO
(WHAM)

ZURU
(SLIP)
BYUN
(WHOOSH)
!!

ZA (STOMP)
ZA

BAGAN
(WHAM)

BASHI
(SMACK)
......
THAT'S BRUTAL...

JUST AS EXPECTED FROM FATHER!

DO
(SLAM)
DO

THIS IS BAD
...

WELL, NOW ...
THIS COULD BE IT...
......

HAA.
ふらっ
FURA (STUMBLE)
HAA.

DOGAA (SHOVE)

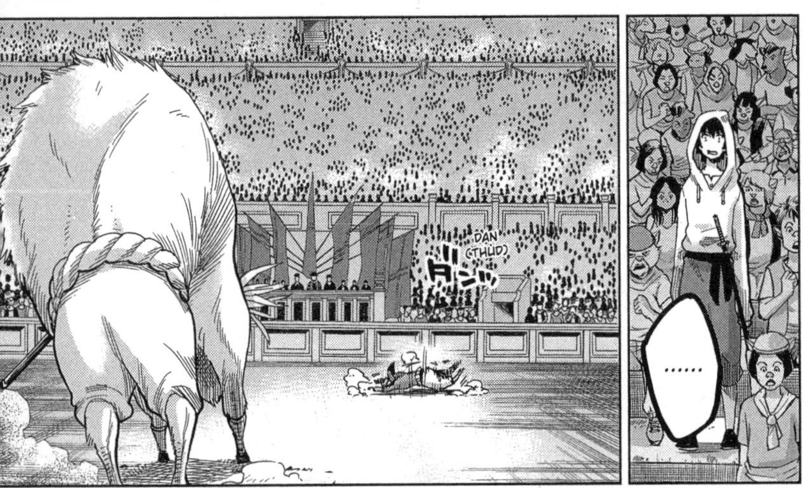
DAN
(THUD)
......

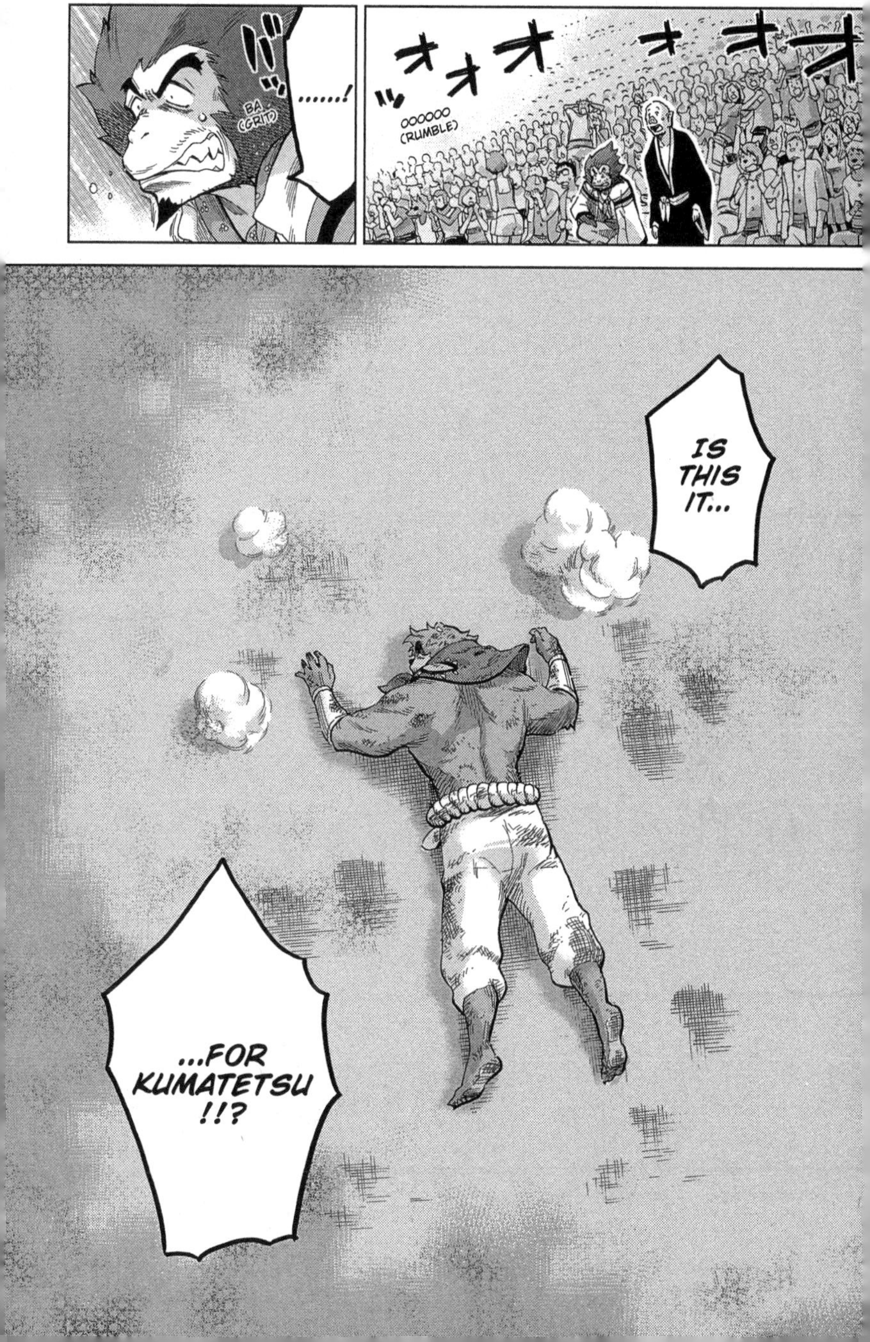

IS THIS IT...

...FOR KUMATETSU !!?

One!

Two!

HE'S GIVING THE COUNT...
IF HE DOESN'T COME BACK TO BEFORE THE COUNT OF TEN...
...IT'S OVER...

Three!
KUMA-TETSUUU!
オオオオ
OOOO (RUMBLE)
ピョコ
PYOKO (PEEK)
KYU...
Four!
EEK!
ダ
DA (DASH)
Five!
BA (WHOOSH)

Six!
DA
DA
DA (THUD)
WAH!
DA
DA
WHAT!?
Seven!

DA
THAT'S...
...KUMA-TETSU'S FIRST DISCIPLE...!?

KYUTA ...!

WHAT DO YOU THINK YOU'RE DOING ...
SUU (BREATHE)
すぅ…
...YOU IDIOT !!?
BACHII (SNAP)
CHAPTER 12 END

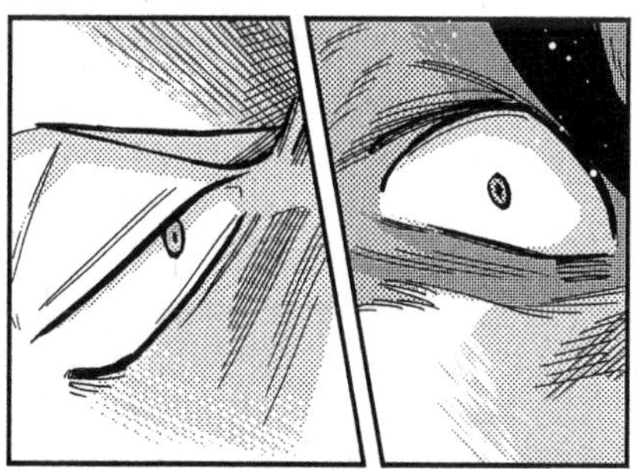

THE BOY & THE BEAST

Chapter 13 MASTER AND DISCIPLE

...
KUMA-
TETSU.

HE
CAME
TO.
MASTER
KUMA-
TETSU!

GUGU
(STRAIN)

SU
(SWISH)

YOU...

AND WHAT ABOUT YOU?

YOU LOOK SO STUPID RIGHT NOW!

IT'S PATHETIC!

ARE THEY REALLY GOING TO HAVE A FIGHT RIGHT NOW!?

KYUTA.

HELP KUMATETSU FIND HIS COURAGE ...!!

DON'T YOU LOSE HEART !!

OR CAN'T YOU FIGHT AT ALL WITHOUT ME!!?

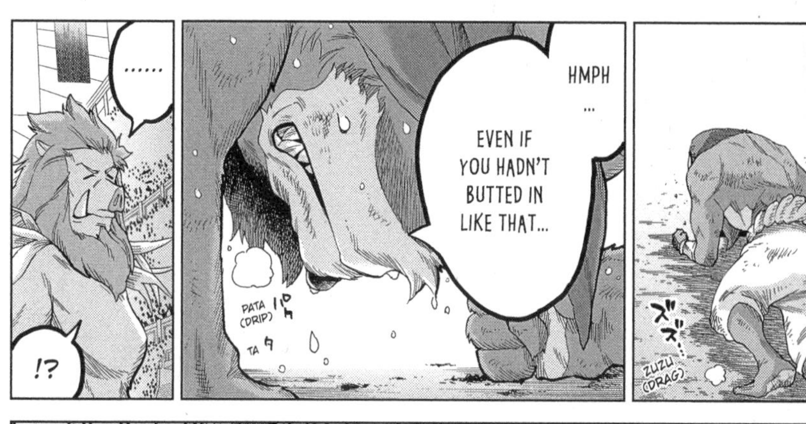

BA (FWIP)

…I WON'T…

…LOSE!

RAAAA...
...A
AA
AAAAAAAAAHHHH!!!!

ZU (JUMP)
BAN (THUD)

DA (DASH)
WHAT !?
TA (THUD)
TA
TA
ZA
ZA
ZU (SKID)
ZA

OOOOOOOOO (RUMBLE)
......

MASTER KUMA-TETSUUUUUU!!
おおおっ!!
OOOOH!
SUTON (THUD)
すとん

THOSE TWO...

OH?
SO HE'S BACK IN THE FIGHT!?

LOOKS LIKE THINGS ARE ABOUT TO GET INTEREST-ING.

ZA
(THUD)
ZA
ZA
ZA
ZA

GIN (CLACK)
ギッ
BUKU (BRISTLE)
ブワッ
GU (GRIP)
ぐっ
YOUR RIGHT!! SWAY!
GASP!
......
!?

HYUN (WHOOSH)

COUNTER!!

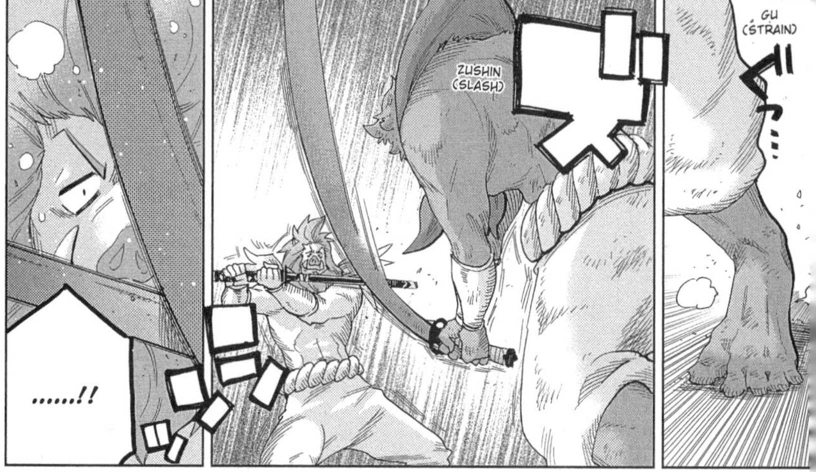

OKAY, YOU GOT THIS!!
CENTER!!!
GIN (CLANK)
UGH...
GIN
GIN
GIN
GIN
GIN

......
TAKE A LOOK AT THAT.
HE'S SMILING...
YEAH...
THAT'S THE FACE HE MAKES WHEN HE'S TRAINING WITH KYUTA.

HE IS IN A STATE OF ABSOLUTE CONCENTRATION.

A PERFECT TRANCE...

KUMATETSU COULD NOT POSSIBLY WIN BY HIMSELF.

HOWEVER ...

IF IT'S THE TWO OF THEM TOGETHER, THEN WHO KNOWS ...!!?

RRAAAAAAAH!!!
GIN (WHACK)
UGH!!!

CLACK
KURU
KURU (TWIRL)
CLACK CLACK
HANG IN THEEEEERE ...
DAD ...!

CLACK
GIRI (GRIND)
GIRI
GUGUGU (STRAIN)
AAAHHH, HE'S GONNA LO—

SILENCE !!
UGH!
ZUI (SHOVE)

KYUTA ...

THAT BASTARD... HE'S JUST A HUMAN ...

BIG BRO...?

UGGGH ...

GIRI

GIRI

DON'T LET HIM PRESS YOU! DON'T YOU LOSE!!

GUH ...
USE...
...YOUR IDIOTIC STRENGTH!
GU (STRAIN)
GU
GYARI (SLIDE)
GASHI (WHACK)

PAKI (CRACK)
PAKI
PAKI
PAKI
PAKI
PAKI
PAAN (SHATTER)
!?
FU (FWIP)
......
WHAT ...?

BASHI (WHACK)

BYUN (WHOOSH)

DAN (THUNK)

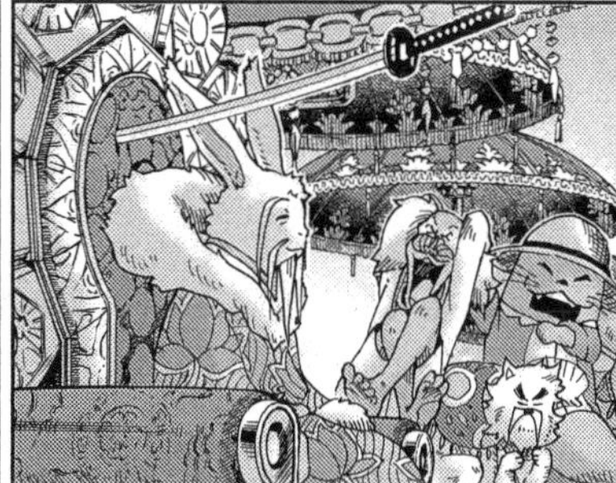

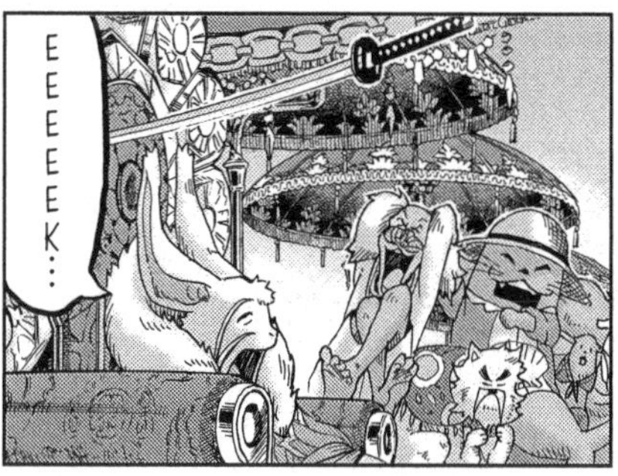

... RIGHT ...

... THERE!

BASHIII
(WHAM)
バシィィ!!

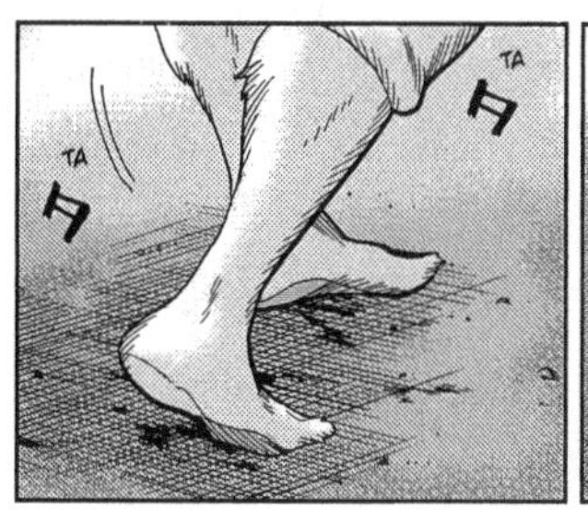

DOSA
(THUD)
ドザッ

One!

Two!

Three!

Four!

Nine!

The winner!
Kuma-
tetsu
!!!!
WAAAAAH!!
CHAPTER 13 END

THE BOY & THE BEAST

WAAH!
パラ
PARA (FLUTTER)
パラ
PARA
パラ
PARA
WAAAAHHH!
UGH ...
BUN (SHAKE)
ぶん
ぶん
BUN

DON'T SCARE ME LIKE THAT.

I NEVER ASKED YA TO WORRY.
...... I CAN'T BELIEVE YOU ACTUALLY WON.
OF COURSE I DID!

......
DON'T BE AN IDIOT. YOU WERE FALLING APART OUT THERE.

SHUT UP.

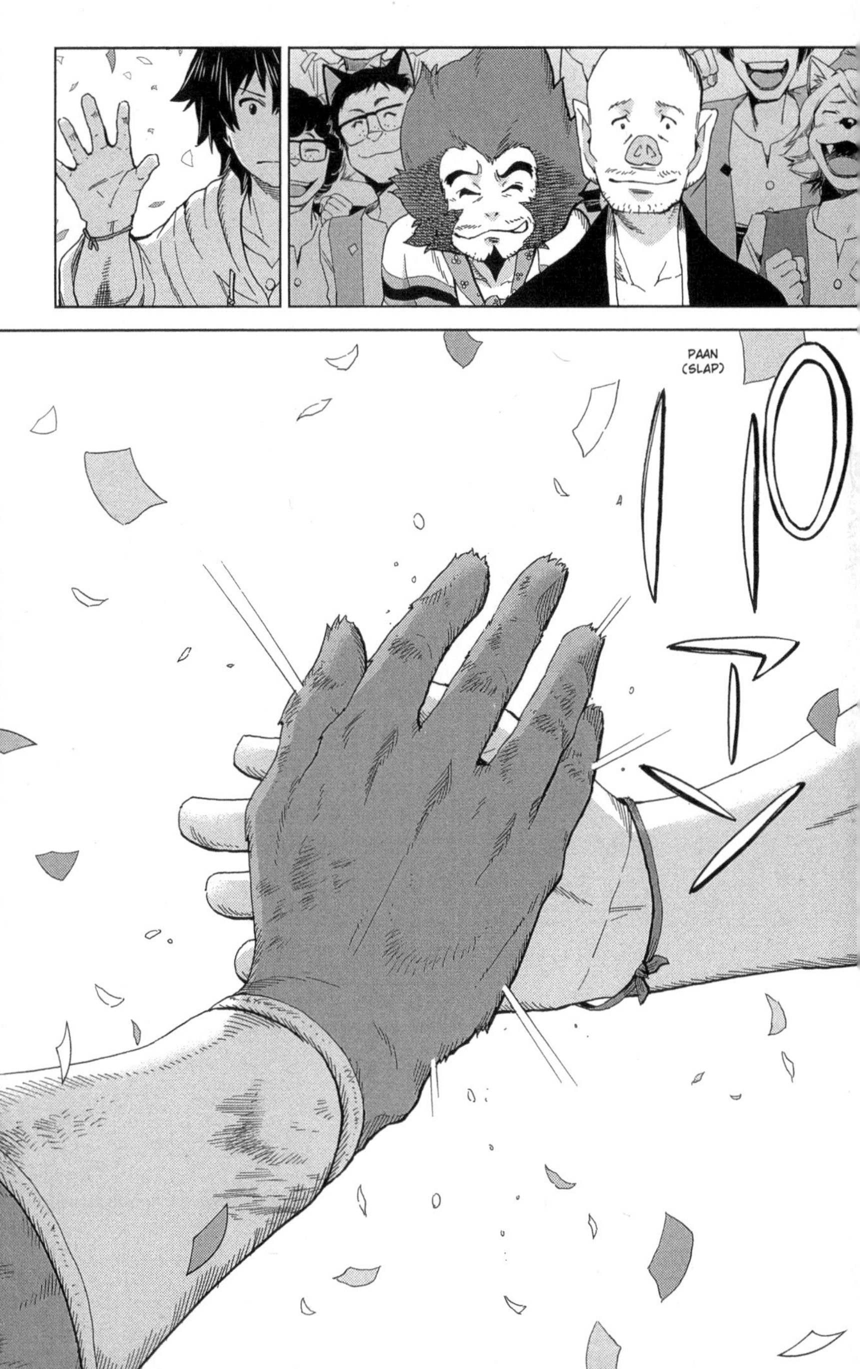
PAAN
(SLAP)
パァン

Chapter 14 FATHERS AND SONS

HEH
HEH
HEH.

THIS IS THE BIRTH OF A NEW LEADER!!

WAAH!

HE'S
A GOOD
SON...

HUH?
LET'S GO.

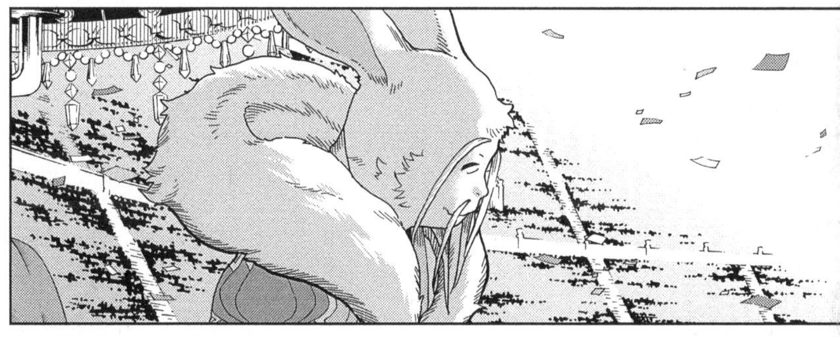

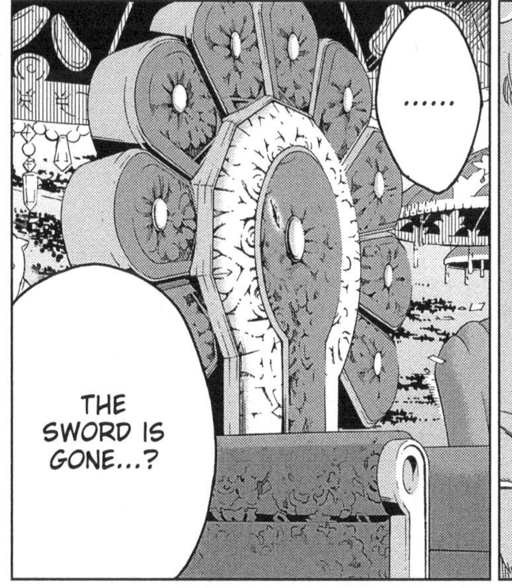
......
THE SWORD IS GONE...?

HYUN (WHOOSH)
OO (FWOOSH)
DO (THUNK)

ZURU (SLIP)
ズル…
HUH …?

KYUTA ...?

TAKE THAT... KYUTA!!!

LOOK!

FATHER ...

I'VE SETTLED THE MATCH WITH YOUR SWORD AND MY TELEKI-NESIS!
......
YOU'VE WON!
WHAT... HAVE YOU DONE ...!?

NOW I'LL FINISH HIM OFF.
FATHER COULDN'T POSSIBLY LOSE TO A HALF-WIT LIKE HIM, OF COURSE!
ZAWA (FSH)

GU (GRIP)
ISN'T THAT RIGHT, KYUTA ...?
パキン
PAKIN (SNAP)
BUKU (WHOOSH)
ISN'T THAT SOOOOOO
OOO
OOO (RUMBLE)
OOO
OOO
OO?

......!
STOP!
ICHIRO-HIKO—!!!
GU (GRAB)
ZURI (STAGGER)

ZAWA (MURMUR)
AAAAAHHHH!
AH—
HA-HA-HA-HA-HA...
GAKUN (SLUMP)
BADADA (DRIP)

MY FATHER, IOZEN, IS THE WINNER !!
HA-HA!
HA!
HA!
HA-HA!
HA.

ZAWA
(RUSH)

OOOH H!
HYUUU (FSSHH)
U
U
K—
KYUTA?
AH!
BA (WHOOSH)
AAAAAHHHH!
GATA (CLATTER)
GATA
GATA
UWGG
GG
GG
......!
YOU MUSTN'T, KYUTA! REJECT THE DARKNESS ...!!

BUCHI (SNAP)
BUCHI
SURAA (SLIDE)
BAN (WHOOSH)

......
STOP, PLEASE ...
KYUTA ...!!!
UWGGGGG
G
DON (WHOOSH)
GGHHH!

KYU!
BA (JUMP)
KYU.
KYU.
KUWA (OPEN)

GASI (CHOMP)
!!

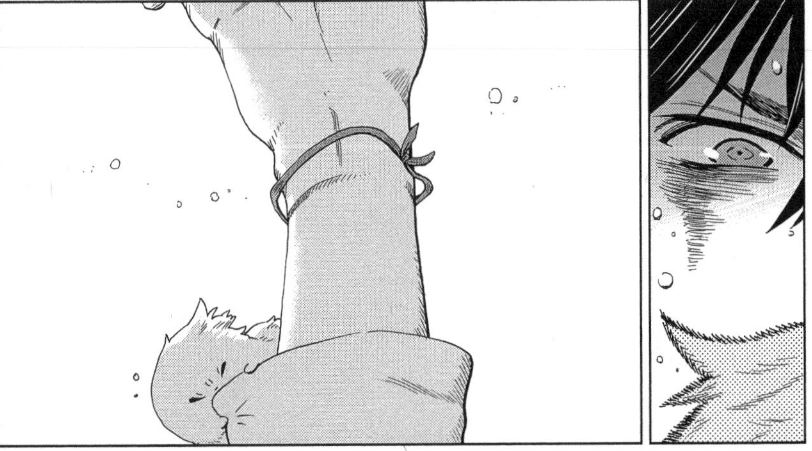

IT'LL PROTECT YOU...

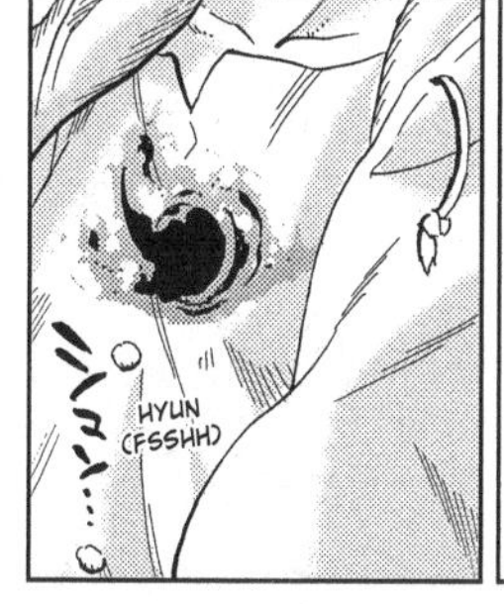

FU (WHISH)

POSU (THUMP)
ボスッ

......
HAA.
HAA.

......
ICHIRO-HIKO.
I'LL NEVER FORGIVE YOU...
...KYUTA...
ZAWA (WHOOSH)
ZAWA
COULD THAT POSSIBLY BE...

... FORGIVE ...
I'LL ...
... NEVER ...
DORO (BUBBLE)
DORO
DORORO
...A MONSTER ...?
GOPO (WHOP)
KYUTA ...
......

HAA.
HAH.
HAA.

WHY ...
... ARE YOU ASLEEP ...?

WAKE
...

...
UP
...!

CHAPTER 14 END

THE BOY & THE BEAST

THANK YOU FOR READING THE THIRD VOLUME OF *THE BOY AND THE BEAST*!

I'm Renji Asai.
About a month after the movie started showing in theaters, they showed a program on TV about Director Hosoda while he was working on *The Boy and the Beast*. I watched it, of course, and I very clearly felt the passion of the entire staff, especially the director.

I personally love drawing expressions, so when I saw just how committed the director was to the expressions of the characters, I felt like, even though we differ in both area of expertise and skill level, I'd found a small commonality between us. That made me very happy.

Now that the manga is nearing its climax, I'm trying to show everything, even the feelings and history behind the expressions.

I hope I can draw a realistic portrayal of things.
There's only one volume left, but I do hope to see you there!

SPECIAL THANKS!
Yuho Ueji-sensei, Akira Katou-san, Yamauchi-san, Maeda-san, Oosako-san, Nagashima-san, Akabane-san, Oohashi-shi, NAOKI, my editor Kousuke Kinoshita-san, my editor Ittoku Kimura-san.
Thank you so much for helping me for so long.

The Bob Boy and the Beast ❸

Original Story *Mamoru Hosoda* · *Art* *Renji Asai*

Translation: ZephyrRZ · Lettering: Bianca Pistillo

Yen Press
1290 Avenue of the Americas
New York, NY 10104

Visit us at yenpress.com
facebook.com/yenpress
twitter.com/yenpress
yenpress.tumblr.com

First Yen Press Edition: March 2017

Library of Congress Control Number: 2015955216

ISBN: 978-0-316-46929-6

10 9 8 7 6 5 4 3 2 1

BVG

Printed in the United States of America